The Canals of Mars

PATRICK MCGUINNESS was born in 1968 in Tunisia. In 1998 he won an Eric Gregory Award for poetry from the Society of Authors and in 2003 he won the Levinson prize for poetry from the Poetry Foundation. His publications include T.E. Hulme's *Selected Writings* (Carcanet/Routledge USA, 1998, 2003), *Maurice Maeterlinck and the Making of Modern Theatre* (Oxford University Press, 2000), *Symbolism, Decadence and the fin de siècle* (University of Exeter Press, 2000), *Anthologie de la poésie symboliste et décadente* (Paris: Les Belles Lettres, 2001) and, with Charles Mundye, an edition of Laura Riding and Robert Graves, *A Survey of Modernist Poetry* (Carcanet, 2002). His Penguin Classics edition of J.-K. Huysmans' *Against Nature* appeared in 2003, and his translation of Mallarmé's *For Anatole's Tomb* (Carcanet/Routledge USA, 2003) was a Poetry Book Society Recommendation. He has written and presented two programmes for BBC Radio 3: *The Art of Laziness* and *A Short History of Stupidity*.

Patrick McGuinness lives in Cardiff, and is a fellow of St Anne's College, Oxford, where he lectures in French.

T0167433

PATRICK McGUINNESS

The Canals of Mars

CARCANET

First published in Great Britain in 2004 by
Carcanet Press Limited
Alliance House
Cross Street
Manchester M2 7AQ

A CIP catalogue record for this book is available from the British Library
ISBN 1 85754 772 1

The publisher acknowledges financial assistance from Arts Council England

Typeset in Bembo by XL Publishing Services
Printed and bound in England by SRP Ltd, Exeter

For Angharad,

Ac yno'r ydwyt tithau – a myfi,
  Am byth yn chwerthin, tewi, a thristáu,
Ac yno mae'r clogwyni, a'r niwl yn niwl,
  A Medi'n Fedi o hyd, ac un ac un yn ddau.

And there you are yourself – and so am I,
  Forever laughing, falling silent, sorrowing,
And there the precipices are and the mist is mist,
  And September is always September, and one and one make two.

(T.H. Parry-Williams, trans. Richard Poole)

Acknowledgements

Many of these poems have been published in the following journals and magazines: *Agenda, The Guardian, The Independent, Leviathan Quarterly, The London Review of Books, New Welsh Review, PN Review* and *Poetry Wales*. Some have also appeared in *New Writing 10*, ed. Penelope Lively and George Szirtes (Picador/ British Council, 2001) and *New Poetries II*, ed. Michael Schmidt (Carcanet, 1999). 'Borders', 'A History of Doing Nothing', 'Bruges' and 'Heard on UN Square' appeared in *Poetry*.

I am grateful to the Society of Authors for an Eric Gregory Award for poetry in 1998, and to *Poetry* and the Poetry Foundation for awarding me the Levinson Prize in 2003.

Contents

Father and Son	9
Borders	10
No	11
The White Place	12
A History of Doing Nothing	13
Morning	15
A View of Pasadena from the Road	16
The Belgiad	17
Bruges	19
Leuven	20
Belgitude	21
A Border Town	22
Glo	23
Cwlwm	24
Two Paintings by Thomas Jones	
I A Wall in Naples	25
II A Street in Naples	25
Vague Terrain	26
Coney Beach	27
Short Life of a Thought	28
The Canals of Mars	29
Ultrasound	30
First Steps	31
Days in the New Country	32
The Fugue	35
'Death whispers softly'	36
Walls	37
Mist in Palo Alto	38
Dust	39
Heard on UN Square	40
The Shuttle	41
Wasps	43
Birthday Poem for Angharad	44
Another Language	45
An Ending	46
Surfers in a Wing Mirror	47
Host Organisms	48
Heroes	49
Not China but Tours	50
The Darkroom	51

The Old Station in Bouillon   53
My Glasgohemia (Fantasy)   54
A Realist Painting   55
Secret Wars   56
Solid Castles in the Air (Erik Satie on his Times)   57
Lull   60

Father and Son

in memory of my father, and in welcome to my son

In the wings there is one who waits to go on,
and another, his scene run, who waits to go.

I would like to think they met; if not here
then like crossed letters touching in the dark;

the blank page and the turned page,
the first and the last, shadows folding

over and across me, in whom they're bound.

Borders

Like a shadow across the eye, or something dark
in the corner of the day, it was always there

never quite pressed against awareness;
grit in the eye, sand in the shoe

a sound framed by a window behind which nothing moved

so the shadow on the lung

darkening the borders of the breath

soon we learned about the spaces without names:
between days as they open out,
seasons as they taper down and out and
        back into themselves again

with the black border we could see the months
go frame by frame

asking what was slow and what slow motion

or

which was sea and which was ocean

sheep know it, the border that has no marking,
        of no one's making,
the field without a fence beyond
        which nothing feels the same

so a word might cross the unfenced border of its meaning

her name for instance

No

The police stations seamless, riveted
and sealed, foreign as spacecraft; still
the place grows around them. Prams
like hotwired cars lie empty on the grass;
past tricolour kerbstones girls push
at invisible winds; sky the colour of armour
and the air muscular with battle.

The slow quotidien burrs in these hives
of negativity. King Billy and Princess Di
rule their dystopia of Rangers clubs and chip shops
in the here and now; the present tense
with counterflow, facing time head-on
as walls face winds, coasts face off the seas,
and lose so slowly it feels like winning.

The White Place

One afternoon we watched a programme on near-death
experiences: a woman tunnelled back through life

to what came after, and was reluctant
to return, since her life paled beside the white place

she'd been pulled back from. Now she lived between the two,
nostalgic for the afterwards she'd died into.

The next day, dozing on a stationary train
you woke and asked the question that had woken

in your mind as if it were on mine: 'The white place'
you asked, 'will anybody else be there?'

I didn't know. I hadn't thought to ask — no one
had — if in the white place we'd be alone

or with other people. You asked about
your friends, if the best of here translates

to there, or if we leave, as we come in, alone.
I still don't know. I think that we are not alone.

I think it less for your sake now than for my own.

A History of Doing Nothing

And who would write it?
                        Its first historians
were bemused: it moved, yes, but imperceptibly;
used Time as action did, took place along
the hours, the days, needing somewhere to unfold
like all the things it wasn't. The instruments
designed to trap it could not keep up;
the mind slid off it like water on an oily cloth.
In photographs it was the shadow that seemed
to leak from motion, so that each moving
thing looked always in the company
of its ghost, its own grey opposite.

In wars, it was inferred from the slack rigging
of the warships, the flotillas nuzzling at their moorings;
Heraclitus knew: into the same nothing
nobody stepped twice. Physics was born
when they found that all things bring
a corresponding nothing into being;
metaphysics when they learned that in
a perfect world each thing done
aspired to the same thing left undone.

Its founding epic still used heroes, battles, temples…
only for the space that lay between them. Events?
no; the gaps that separate events,
the hungerless white dreams between awakenings,
slow afternoons that ran aground on boredom.
Its sacred books, pristine from inattention,
promised a paradise where all the squandered energy,
dissipated talents, missed appointments
with destiny or with friends would fuse
in one infinity of cancellation;
where not to have been born was only second best.

What of the doers of nothing?
                              To the naked eye
they seemed no different from ourselves, surveyed
the low comedy that was activity from beds
or armchairs, suspended in their dusky lives
as the world turns in the emptiness that holds it steady.
Like us, they folded back into Time's pleats
before going, traceless, where the dead go,
soft-footed in the unresisting dark.

Morning

One house
     next
next again
         pert green
lawn
   white garage
sprinkler   muted

nothing
   out of order   no
 thing
   untoward

wraparound   sound, sigh

of fridge door

   city tightening

the mountains
     seem not to move
         have texture

pavement empty, road adrift, the car
shining safely

the neighbour hood coming to a slow

     coming to a rolling

         boil

A View of Pasadena from the Road

Hell too has its circles. Rounding coils of freeway,
we pass sponsored walls and billboards,
their majestic slogans sliding off the eye.
Hyperbole, free-market capitalese,

a landscape of six-foot letters rewinds
in the tinted glass. As the car scans
the barcode of the road, the ground
evaporates beneath our feet; pavements

roll by unwalked, the traffic tightens
in our throat. So much to see, so little
that holds attention. It is noon

all day, and the shadowless earth
is as thirsty as Mars. In the distance,
the soft porch light of the good life.

The Belgiad

Caesarean state:
every roadsign a mirror
every town a suburb

★

Magritte's Saturn: all rings and no planet

the ever-provisional
coastline dreaming of sea

★

Maigret's Liège stands in for itself
its anonymous crimes
sweepings from the poorhouse floor

Charleroi's slow factories turn like the Ferris
wheel in *The Third Man*

★

Louvain, Gand, Anvers
river-cities face to face with themselves
Leuven, Gent, Antwerpen

Bruges one long aftermath, held breath

★

Bouillon to Blankenberg,
Martelange to Knokke
300 kilometres of frontier
united and untied

★

From the citadel of Namur, Baudelaire's Paris
appears in a cityscape by Rops: France doubled,

doubly not. The Meuse rolls through
as many names as it has valleys to run dry in.

★

All has that faint emphasis, as if the place were in italics,
could look like elsewhere yet be nowhere else.

Bruges

The streets reappear in the water's backwash
of disclosure; brick by widowed brick
houses from Atlantis gaze back: mirage
or mirror image? The real and the reflected

swap dimensions; the swan signs the surface
in his careful hand, neck and neck with his ghost.
Prosperous trees count their leaves;
the canal is calm as it multiplies the dawns.

Leuven

The beguinhof's pink brick, its labyrinthine
paths and winding waterways: a village
modelled on the human heart, a beating
maze of convolutions; each inhabitant

a thought, each visitor the flicker
of an instinct, a reflex in the city's
lapping introspection. All is analogy,
everything is sensed first as something else:

feelings drift by on their way elsewhere,
amble into view on a tide of vagueness,
like disconnected household objects
breasting the water in a flooded house.

The river crumples in an aquatic frown;
something dark passes in the drifting sky;
trees take root in cloud; the town
is clenched around the river it flows by.

Belgitude

I spent autumn learning about autumn,
that its unmistakable confusion about what it was
was what made it what it was. So with Belgium.
It was the first post-national state; wars
came there to be fought, got tired and moved on.
Surveys showed that most Belgians questioned

would have preferred to be from somewhere else:
truly this was home, I thought, all the more
so as home had been a drain on my awareness,
took a little more of me away from me each year.
I came to it side-on, as one climbs into a moving bus;
discovered the world was a small town, or

at any rate vice versa. Soon I learned
to keep my mouth shut in two languages;
I called home on lobster telephones
in a hail of bowler hats. Trains ran on time,
travelling micro-distances in decades.
After a while I fitted in, by looking out of place,

swept into a street-long tidal wave of curtain lace.

A Border Town

This isn't where you'd start by looking:
where big things have tapered down
to feel their way into small lives being led
far away from where you'd think to look,

but where your looking leads. It's where
events have come to hide away, to break,
like light, into those particles of dust that spin
and settle back in layers on what they lit.

Glo

Glo, dark as the place it came from; coal
blazing underground, ponies drawing shoals
of barges along the oily waterways:
canals dreaming of the open seas,

of coal that eddied into coral as
the Mersey flowed into the Meuse.
The tugboats swayed in the gloom, prows
sucking estuary mud, the engine's slow

coal thrum; coal from the Afan
to the citrus groves of Pont Aven;
coal into charcoal; coal into karandash,

a diamond dragging fire across the skies.
Now only afterglow: burned to ash
what once was thunder for the eyes.

Glo: Welsh for coal

23

Cwlwm

Cwlwm was the knot the language had me in,
the tangle-throated syllables of villages and streets;
I saw double before I learned to see them twice.
Then the roadsigns started to take root,

the place-names lifted off the letters
that composed them as in films the spirit
leaves the body. *Calon* into *canol*,
heart into centre, fluent as a stencil

peeling back to leave itself behind.
Adar, aderyn were the birds Clément
Ader's aeroplane translated – the word's
idea of flight joined coast to coast

in the dangerous, sustaining air.
Now from the *geiriadur* the words take off,
the dictionary empties page by page,
letter by letter, column by column.

Welsh words: *cwlwm*: knot; *calon*: heart; *canol*: centre; *adar/aderyn*:
bird/birds; *geiriadur*: dictionary

Two Paintings by Thomas Jones

I *A Wall in Naples*

I look and look until the nothing that I see
perfects itself. I perfect its lack of interest,
as if to show how it would not exist
were I not here to see it (though people see

it every day): a wall in Naples, cracked
plaster and beneath it brick, a horizontal
line of balcony, some hanging clothes racked
along a clothesline, and above it, pale

and ordinary blue, the sky. It's nothing –
it blocks the view; then, as I'm looking,
it becomes the view: in front of me, time's slack,
the world's swerve painted as it turns its back.

II *A Street in Naples*

This is at least release from grander themes;
instead of druids traipsing sullen waterfalls,
bards gazing at their faces mirrored in the sky,
this is an image taken from life's seams,

life's secret pocket, its false-bottomed case:
the things we look at but don't think to see,
the engine room that breathes the spirit of the place.
A real subject inhabiting imagined space,

passed over, lost, forgotten… finds itself
perfected in an image of itself:
the roadside scale of things, a pavement's curb
which as we look becomes the known world's curve.

Vague Terrain

This was always nether-country: a border-
land of empty paint cans, burned-out cars,
dumped fridges cooling in the shade.
A stonehenge of yellowing white goods,
its mysterious circles were understood
only by fly-tippers and their drive-by gods:
Currys, Homebase, Argos.

Their acts of worship were secretive.
They were persecuted but undeterred.
The soil was slow to claim their offerings:
their libations stained the ground,
their breath took breath from the earth around.
They left skeletal metal, statueless plinths,
and beyond them, city walls that gleamed like teeth.

Coney Beach

They mirror mines – mines now gone or bleeding
back into the ground they plumbed. Their rusting
wheels and pulleys find their echo or their after-

lives in rollercoasters, Catherine Wheels,
Big Dippers hauling kids up to the sun
on wings of steel. (The steelworks too are gone.)

Arcades unscramble their electric babel:
pinball murmurings, sweet robotic nothings.
At one-armed bandits men rattle chump change,

their slack hours hanging like oversized coats;
time passes through them like rope through a knot.
Penny-drops fidget with chance, their shanks

of coinage the day's catch glittering out to sea.
The ring of light around the funfair is recession's
dirty tidemark; the sand, its whispering retreats,

the sea that hesitates, turns back,
thinks better of its second thoughts, draws
each breath of shingle as if it were the last.

On the carousel time pivots and remakes
itself at the slot of a coin, the drop of a token,
the point of a unicorn's horn.

At night tattoos sink back to needlepricks,
the skin to its separately bottled inks,
lost colours the day borrowed to shine.

The surf frets at the pier; brimful bins
imagine landfill paradise;
broken glass feeds light to dying suns.

Short Life of a Thought

                         : it starts, mist on a roll
of film, a shell's rumour of the dim remembered
            sea. But it doesn't yet exist,
being a thought unhad, a memory
            of something not yet known;
clay before flesh, sunlight burning off the fog.

Not yet itself: a flickering pilot light, a meteor's
            dead surface pocked
with DNA. Life's tiny intimations. And so it grows,
            mind-muscle in flex,
learning limit as breached limit.
            All things feed and drive it.
It puts down roots; embedded,

it sends out branches, swallows the air,
            converts the space around into versions
of itself; moves in analogy, correspondence,
            devours its like, devours likeness,
creates nothingness in its image; is for a time
            the very force that made it;

forges itself, forgets its madeness
            (but that is part of it,
to forget itself). An element, it thinks itself indivisible,
            the mind's shadowless white noon.
Top-heavy, it commands; all is vista,
            subjugated view.
Day breaks everywhere at once.

All is passed through the thought:
            earth through the worm,
sun through the prism of the thought;
            then is an empire losing hold;
competes with itself for stillness, to stay,
            and with itself to go on; teetering pinnacle,
next self swallowing the last:

The Canals of Mars

Percival Lowell, who in 1895 observed Martian civilisation dying in a great drought, mapped the drying canals of Mars. Lowell believed the earth would go the same way.

*The scene is Mars, whose raw unnatural clouds
unfurl across red dawns: Martians pass
from camp to receding camp, their country
diminishing so fast beneath their feet
it is like snow thawing on the prairie.*

★

It could be us, but not yet...
from his observatory he spies
the Martian tribes following canals
across the thirsty Martian
earth to their extinction.

For them he has imagined the most improbable,
most protracted tragedy: the planet's
unslakable red thirst and the hordes kept moving
in the fiery night. He can imagine their suffering,
but cannot imagine *them*.

In dreams it is the swaddled Martian papoose
who comes to him, with his Martian mother
in her ripped space-moccasins, dried-
out and hankering, as Martians hanker,
inscrutably, without expression.

They have no features yet to fix their pain
into. Their mute suffering feeds on itself
like the thirst that wrings their bodies
dry, who even as they move become the
dust, feet battering the sand in noiseless bursts.

Ultrasound

I

Noiseless swirls of dark.
Then a flash, a white zodiac.

He is like morning:
flesh, a body dawning;

his skeleton a silver filament,
his body a bulb in a roomful of night.

II

The Plough stalls on black acres, furrows
tilled and seeded; the earth broken
where the star baby turns and grows.

A first page dropping anchor in the ink.

First Steps

for Holly

or   the next
already out of sight
sure as tomorrow's weather?

first step: arms out for
is it the falling walls
the floor rising to hold you

in your one-piece tiger suit
roaming the plains
of hessian

tiny giant strides; you cross
the room, moon–dust
or is it talc between your toes

Days in the New Country

Newborn beings emerge from the Arrivals
lounge, sniffer dogs and luggage snapping
at their ankles. Behind plate-glass walls, streets

sway in the heat, breathe like faraway furnaces.
Passports stamped, beyond the sliding door
visa, vista: both lay the country at your feet.

★

Along broad avenues the trees
are on patrol, portraits of the Leader
like lopped heads cradled in their branches.

Loudspeakers murmur slogans for the ear
to slide off. In the spaces between trees,
guard dogs doze beside spectacular militia.

★

The year peters out into a tail of power failures,
food shortages, a detritus of old calendars,
unfindable spare parts for broken Chinese toys.

Always a street away, Orthodox chant;
incense tracing prayer's trajectory, making prayer
visible, as dust brings out an arc of light.

★

Then the season of frozen fountains;
the Boulevard of Socialist Victory
in perpetual mid-construction.

Gypsies beg, are beaten and moved on;
no one cares, they don't exist: optical illusions,
revenants, the sleeve-tugging of gone days.

★

The waitress in the pirated Coke T-shirt
that reads *You Can't Stand the Feeling!*
recites the menu like a roll-call of extinct species.

In the Natural History Museum
the extinct species are making room.
Birds are silent by the treeful.

★

Never so little sign of so much to come.
Events hold their breath, as if unsure whom
to happen to. Then they're overtaken by events:

the Ceausescus standing on their balcony
as the cheering turns to jeering. To them
both looked the same; too high to tell
how power spares the powerful the very
understanding that might spare them.

★

A week takes place in spurts, like the newsreel
footage of the ransacked ministries,
broken statues, the teargas that unleashed
the tears that bubbled up through cobbles,
feathered up from drains and hydrants,
from the cracked tarmac of the motorways
to the crazy paving of the presidential palace.

Underneath the flagstones is the beach.

★

The trial is filmed inside a bunker:
he puts out a grainy hand to guide her

through the darkness. Later, slumped
against the wall, their faces are composed;

the backs of their heads lie beside
them like a dropped disguise.

The revolution is a slipped mask.
They are free to be themselves at last.

The Fugue

T.W. Adorno writes of a Bach fugue: 'It is an art of dissection; one could almost say, of dissolving Being, posited as the theme, and become incompatible with the common belief that this Being maintains itself static and unchanged throughout the fugue.'
    'Bach Defended Against his Devotees'

Microscopic: a maze of cells around
        A spreading core of sound,
Lost in a gallery of its reflections;
Loosening as it holds, one small motif
For DNA, maps itself, as a leaf
Maps out the tree it is and grows upon.

The mind sways, while its hazy metaphor,
        The body, feeds on air,
Heals casually as it fills out its skin.
Never the Many binding into One:
The flax unwinds, the braiding comes undone,
From cell to lonely cell the atoms spin.

The fugue is not the Many striving for
        The One, binding from their
Broken parts a whole that never can grow
Less, or grow less plentiful. Seen backwards,
The parts are what the whole is drawn towards:
By now the centre's pull seems tired, slow,
        Though all the pieces fit
It is the playing grows disconsolate.

In minute revolutions it maintains,
        First, how the centre strains
But holds, as a drop of water fattens
On an edge of light; or else it mirrors
Release, disintegration, the mirrors
Drained of their reflections, and the patterns
        Of your voice escaping you;
Explaining what, they ask, consoling who?

'Death whispers softly'

Death whispers softly: 'I am no one,
I do not even know myself:
the dead do not know they are dead,
nor even that they are dying –
children at least, or heroes, the sudden deaths.

My beauty is made up
of last moments – lucidity, a face –
the beauty of what would be me
without me. For as soon as I am
(that one dies) I cease to be.

Thus am I made of forebodings,
intuitions, supreme shudders.
I am not except in idea.

As for the others, for the living,
their tears, their mourning, etc.,
that is just my shadow clothing them in black.'

After Mallarmé's notes for *Anatole's Tomb*

Walls

Lleyn

stone lodged on stone noun on noun
for mortar live air   dry breath
and on the other side
sky   sheep   sea   sun sinking and rising

the day in pieces   irregular
half stone   half hole
half view   half held from view

unwatched they brace the wind   divide
the onslaught

                        bind what harms them into
                        sustaining patterns of
                        mute resistance

Mist in Palo Alto

Headlamps burning
      deep as bronze in firelight
            cars tipping into night

the freeway numb with mist
      all-night traffic stalled
            a far-off muffled waterfall

road signs cat's eyes
      cancel themselves out
            mildew damp bark eucalyptus

press in over
      the dashboard's vanilla stay fresh
            cold spray closing over

too late now
      to turn back
            to push on

Dust

Form and form-giver, light and light-bearer,
mistaken for air, for light by the eye,
flies wingless, lighter than what it bears

Stored in the eye, makes sight substance,
guides the pen, the brush, thickens dimensions;
shorelines hinge on it, feathers aspire to it

Form and form-giver, translates the sun
a bauble turns it and turns in it
leaves coil in it, shine like coins in it

disappears and is lighter than disappearance

Heard on UN Square

'The first move makes the game'
        is the word on the street: the chess players
on UN Square know it, sitting face
        to face, lost in one another's thoughts

★

'Man, MAN' he asks, 'you think
        you need to *be* somewhere?'
His lazy eye divides you right:
        three parts habit, one part fear

★

So thin, she says, 'you can't say
        if they or their shadows were there first'
then is gone, stepping sideways
        into the next moment, the next thirst

★

Running on the spot, all he has is 'now':
        those blank time-acres hour after hour.
The shop dummies in the windows,
        'like soap stars between shows'

★

The ragged dandy always looks his best,
        small proprieties that seem to say:
'I have now washed and dressed
        and have gone north into the day'

★

Another day filled with himself.

Hands out, hands again, strange
coincidence of two needs: 'change'

The Shuttle

That swollen winter lying glandular
in my half-hallucinated rain-forest
of a bedroom, I watched myself drifting
to the window on a tide of perspiration.
Pyjamas like cling film, eyelids in flames,
I tuned in and out of the fever they thought
would *take me* – *where* I never knew,
nobody said, I was just the passenger
and this the tropical winter of my brush with
(low whispers) *what comes after*, something dim
I knew I touched but could not see.

Alone for hours I watched the shuttle graze
its night-acres, padding the black obsidian
fields of space to the echoes of long gone,
still-reverberating blasts; I heard white noise,
saw blackouts, ran my mind along the edge
of placeless voices calling *lift off and do you read…*

                   … for weeks, my fever
was the shadow of that shuttle, the story
of the fire that drove it on and up.
I dreamed I ran the cratered prairies
of the moon; in slow motion or at the speed
of light Christmas came and went,
people moved like wallpaper through the room.
Their shadows stayed long after they were gone.

             In my bloated head I screened
replay after replay of take-off, watched
as in mid-air the shuttle hung like a lobbed
newspaper frozen in its arc, cast half
its body aside in a blaze of fire; then,
rising, kicked it back, threw off its earthly self
and as I too rose it was like stripping off
my life in layers;

I unlocked the ceiling,
head burning, face on fire, my twelve years
the debris that fell back, the chaos
I climbed free of as I walked on air,

and woke weeks later to find myself still here.

Wasps

It was vinegar, we thought, not honey
Inside the hanging nest, just out of sight,
That beat for weeks above the balcony.
The pounding heart they shared was quiet

Only when it slept. All day they threaded
Through white noise, their sullen waspish muzak.
Moving, they dissected movement, spread
Along the air like muscle underneath

The skin. At night the house became our hive,
The rooms and corridors unfolding
Spectacularly for us as we lived
Unseen behind a window that had grown

A soundless fur of wasps. Soft undersides,
Bright balls of anger suddenly uncurled,
Became deliberate and slow, intent
On warmth; harmless until daylight hurled

Them back into the vortex of their noise.
Months later, having lived in droves, they died
In ones and twos. We found the nest, an eyeless
Skull still breathing, with next year's wasps in sight.

Birthday Poem for Angharad

The window gives no clue.
Outside, the sun could be
another season's, but for the
cold you cannot see; the branching
cracks along the sky are tensed

to hold it up. Things lock their edges
into light. This arbitrary day
you'll fill out with yourself, as through
the moving glass you see the trees
are rooted in clear air.

Another Language

Writing was to build on paper;
To speak was to make things out of air;
To see was to take light and shape it
Into something that was never there.

An Ending

Love, the small word, the search for better
comes back to this. Or, loved, four

years on that one word's even keel
before the journey ends, before in turn

we realise we haven't moved. Maybe
all have this, and maybe all uniquely

celebrate it. From weakness, from
love, to run up against this both

meeting and collision is to return.
Light, bright air, no breeze: suddenly,

our not moving is what dizzies, not our speed.

Surfers in a Wing Mirror

Closing on Rest Bay, we see the surfers,
        half-boy, half board, sea-centaurs
scaling rolling waterwalls. They live for waves,
        for rumours of waves,
cresting the water's rise and fall, ridging
        hills of spume, water-
mountaineers borne up by what consumes them:
        fall;

driving past we watch them disappear,
        distorted in the wing mirror's
mannered version of themselves; arms
        at right angles to their torsos,
a marine rodeo of elongated limbs
        whose foam and water horses
run themselves into the sand. Matter
        clothing energy,

half bodies now, half forms of thought,
        a revolution of the waves:

insurgents storming barricades of air

Host Organisms

an exhibition of medical photographs

A history of the symptom, the forgotten
Sufferer its playground, illnesses once
Called 'the body's secret festivals'
(Maeterlinck) in mid–celebration here:

Counterpoints of suppurating open
Sores, cracked skin, dead flesh, telescoping
In on new geographies, new maps, new
Trammelled surfaces of waste as bodies

Die to their unbridled final flings.
'When disease enters the body' (Goncourt
Brothers, 1862), 'a stranger
Makes the place his own'.

                    This exhibition
Is that stranger's new biography, though
The premises he commandeers go
Unrecorded. 'Syphilis: second stage'

Reads one such occupation: an impassive
Man holds out a mountain range of chancres,
Dying flesh mined for some new volcanic
Ore. 'Alienation', 'Epilepsy',

'Nymphomania', 'Dyspepsia'…
Nameless faces of the barely-there,
The partly-there, the human background, diseased
Until Disease becomes their *raison d'être*,

Their claim upon the new technology
Of the objective. Charcot holds up the pale
wrist of 'Locomotive Ataxia':
A woman in profile, face melting as

A shadow fills the empty socket of
Her eye. For most of them this was their first
And only chance to meet photography:
Host organisms to more famous guests.

Heroes

I think the sun, the moon
and some of the stars are
kept on their tracks
by this Person's equilibrium
   Lil, in Ed Dorn's *Gunslinger*

That 'some' – *only* some – that measure in all
things, even when the praise outsoars the praised
but is never good enough, still falls
short though it takes in a world, entire skies

to give the airy Slinger ballast
and close his image in her words. Un-
bridled praise, but she holds back: no limits,
only frontiers for this superhuman

cowboy, slender in the sunlight of her eye.
Red suns burn to white. As she sees him leave,
saddling his talking horse, she thinks he'll fly
to join the things she can compare him with.

Not China but Tours

I said I would not fly again
for quite a bit. I did not know
William Empson, 'Autumn on Nan Yueh'

'If flight's as general as this'
      Wrote Empson ('Autumn on Nan Yueh')
His England telescoping in,
      His Europe dimming as he flew…
The landing gave flight's valences
      Perspective, opened them to view,
So that his restless meditation
      On what we fly from, flying to,
Sliced itself against both edges
      Of a single impulse (that left two).
He walked on – his sands were shifting –
      Mine are sticking to my shoe.

'I have flown here, part of the way':
      My bed–desk–lamp triumvirate,
Four walls and window framing sky,
      Are the arena for the measured
Taking stock, the long-delayed
      Landing I had hoped to profit by.
And in a sense it works, though my
      Flight (Air France), and my flight, postdate
Too much the things I fly away
      From, arriving here too late,
Wrong knots tied, right ones still to tie
      And the familiar mess in wait.

The Darkroom

The relatives could not recognise their dead from photographs
H.B., photographer at the Paris Morgue, *c.* 1890

His first photograph was a building site in mid-
construction. Whether the *Rue impériale* stands
ruined or in process, he cannot any longer tell.
The shutter has stayed open a full half-hour,
drinking in the street it emptied. The people
are invisible, who as they move make
no impression on the copper plate.

This, he thinks, is how ghosts are born.

★

He could be fishing for shapes, the room
could be a coastal shelf at night, quiet
in the aftermath of some catastrophe.
The sea could be a darkroom,

where black water licks its banks and waits.
Something lost, forgotten, puts on body
as he sifts among the wreckage. His hands
are nets, drag spectral bodies, faces lost to night.

★

Not dead: asleep. The camera can euphemise
as much as language, as much as death
can put on shapes of sleeping, seem
temporary, hold its own reality at bay…

… thinking it would never be like this,
that his work was all creation, fixing living
people, things blazing in their worlds,
and his artless art uncovering the known,

making as it found. The families could not *see*,
their own dead were drained of all resemblance:
backlit vanishings, abstracted bodies; the world
was healing over them, was growing back.

The Old Station in Bouillon

after a line by Valery Larbaud

Such travels, Cosmopolitan of the local line!
They've put you out to pasture in a meadow
of iron and steel. Your waiting room waits,
whose double doors once opened on the globe.

The tannoy mouths the silent station names:
Paliseul, Virton, Bertrix, each one like you
a terminus. The thrum of faraway
goodbyes… the leavetakings, the homecomings,

are the shadow of a shudder on the rails.
The rust will stay in bloom, and you
will taste the seasons as they pass through.

My Glasgohemia (Fantasy)

after Rimbaud

Away I'd go, tuffies stuffed into burst pockets;
My anorak too became ideal;
I'd cruise the low sky for you Musey! I was your feral
Servant, and what splendid loves I recked!

My only breeks had a hole big enough for two.
– Daydreaming tomcat, I thumbed
My rhyming guidebook. On Ursa Major I bummed
A few nights' kip. – My stars rustled in their sky,

And as those bountiful September nights dripped
Dew on my napper, bracing as a giddy nip,
I'd listen, bare-arsed on the kerbside where I'd start,

Right there, to rhyme among fantastic shades,
Twanging the elastic lyre of my knackered blades,
One foot on the starting block, ready at my heart!

A Realist Painting

Who are they? What do they see?

The man is neat, aspiring; his look
the painting's organising principle.
She looks elsewhere, though there is nowhere else:
eye to eye with the camera, brow to brow
with the brush, the canvas contemplates itself:

the world is naked as a cracked code,
the street is billed and boarded, brand names
trademarking the air. Underfoot, the polished
cobbles show the scene in convex, their rough squares
making a mosaic of the picture they are a part of.

Secret Wars

We know the sick:
our doubles, ourselves glimpsed
as on another track.

We see their backs; staying,
they pass by. Even
here they are going,

are already gone. We see our-
selves in them; they only
see themselves in our

unseeing eyes; they watch us
watching as the shadow
that they throw invades them.

Solid Castles in the Air (Erik Satie on his Times)

People used to say to me: 'Wait until you're fifty, then you'll see.' I am fifty. I haven't seen anything.
                    Erik Satie

I

Think how his supple, seated frame fills out
            its meticulous black suit;
and how the sleeves begin, unseen, to sprout
            intricately into hands,
how they so tenuously start to flout
            introversion's unilateral rules, expand
on loneliness in tonal sarabandes,

transfer crisp arabesques on air
            that like ivy curl
around the unseen columns
            of his solitude,
transcribe the patterned rows of birds
            on telegraph wires
or charm the backlit hieroglyphs from their
            cages into sound.

II *A Late Arrival*

They buried it, along with an anthology
Of its favourite possessions, and a few
Smells to give it ballast. 'Pince-nez', the
Sculpted beard, the ivory-tipped cane;
The absinthe fumes and smoke from cigarettes –
The age disappears behind particulars, the place
Dams up behind the welter of the details
It produced. A Paris locked inside its
Image, and I missed it, suitcase in hand,
As one misses trains, suitcase in hand:
Last songster of these decomposing times, this
Fleshing out between high-points of bone.
Now the gaps are all that matter,
My only matter. And music? 'Free of Time'

They say, because it fabricates its own,
Makes up the rules it keeps to as it goes along.

III

Hard to be nostalgic, not having invested
in anything to remember; having only ever
lived the life to come, and always, as a promise
to myself, ahead of myself. But no soul
is certain that it has no need to rise,

occasionally, 'symbolically', to elegise
an age that weaned it even in its passing by.
I join the dots until they too disappear: notes
that swivel on their axes and fold back into
pleats of air – their only footholds, their occasions.

IV

So still and resolutely *maudit*:
nothing, these limbs without a body,

this pose, tended so carefully to dispose
of itself between acts. Saint-Saëns

(*La République*) at regimental
ease, the orchestra at roll-call,

stiffened ranks of the *conservatoire*,
wooden batons churning empty air

like milk until it curdles in the bell-
dome of their medalled concert-hall.

Their carrots and their sticks, their small heroics
unclimb the scale in sleepy acrobatics.

Let me pitch the airy tent of *my* conservatory,
    and down a disappearing path of sound
a void takes place beneath a scaffolding of tune.

V

The arms have tunnelled through the sleeves,
The sleeves have sprouted into hands,
The hands have parted into fingers and
    the fingers into keys.

The player folds into the jaws of the piano.

Lull

Tropical and slow, the suburbs
loosen in the tilting sun:
everything is possible, has stopped,
is finished and about to happen.